Blue wildebeests in the
Liuwa Plain National Park

NATIONAL
GEOGRAPHIC
KiDS

RISE OF THE LIONESS

RESTORING A HABITAT AND ITS PRIDE ON THE LIUWA PLAINS

BRADLEY HAGUE

NATIONAL GEOGRAPHIC

WASHINGTON, D.C.

For Emily

Copyright © 2016 Bradley Hague

Special thanks to Matthew Becker, Graeme Ellis, Fynn Corry, and Vera Hoffman from the Zambian Carnivore Programme; Rob Reid and Cynthia Walley from African Parks.

Published by National Geographic Partners, LLC.
Since 1888, the National Geographic Society has funded more than 12,000 research, exploration, and preservation projects around the world. The Society receives funds from National Geographic Partners, LLC, funded in part by your purchase. A portion of the proceeds from this book supports this vital work. To learn more, visit www.natgeo.com/info.

For more information, visit www.nationalgeographic.com, call 1-800-647-5463, or write to the following address:
National Geographic Partners, LLC
1145 17th Street N.W.
Washington, D.C. 20036-4688 U.S.A.

Visit us online at nationalgeographic.com/books

For librarians and teachers: ngchildrensbooks.org

More for kids from National Geographic:
kids.nationalgeographic.com

For information about special discounts for bulk purchases, please contact National Geographic Books Special Sales: ngspecsales@ngs.org

For rights or permissions inquiries, please contact National Geographic Books Subsidiary Rights: ngbookrights@ngs.org

NATIONAL GEOGRAPHIC and Yellow Border Design are trademarks of the National Geographic Society, used under license.

Designed by Callie Broaddus

Text is set in ITC Giovanni Std.
Headers and captions are set in Knockout.

Hardcover ISBN: 978-1-4263-2532-8
Reinforced library edition ISBN: 978-1-4263-2533-5

Printed in Hong Kong
16/THK/1

The people who live around Liuwa Plain National Park largely make their living by fishing.

TABLE OF CONTENTS

INTRODUCTION

"Be careful in the morning," they said. "Sometimes the lions come into camp."

I had traveled around the world to see the famed Lady of Liuwa (Le-YOO-ah) and her small family of lions up close. Having them wandering into camp, I thought, was probably too close. But on the third day at Matamanene Bush Camp, that's exactly what happened. Lady, three lion cubs, and the cubs' mother, Sepo, walked right past the front door of our tent and wandered around the camp. Then, after finding nothing to entertain them, they headed back out to the plains. There, Lady began to hunt two wildebeests all alone.

Lions are the most social of cats and almost always live and hunt in groups known as prides. The prides are key to a lion's success. The way they hunt, the way they live, the way they play—everything in a lion's world revolves around its pride. The idea of a sole lioness taking down a massive bull wildebeest would seem impossible, but not for Lady. She'd done it before. For more than ten years, Lady was a lioness without a pride, a last queen trying to survive in a fallen kingdom. She had to hunt her own food and defend her kills—and had to do so utterly alone.

Today Liuwa seems like a pristine wilderness. It is not. There are tens of thousands of wildebeests where there used to be hundreds of thousands, and there's a handful of cheetahs where there should be dozens. And where lions should reign supreme, they are at risk.

I'd come to Liuwa Plain National Park, in Zambia, Africa, to meet this legendary lioness, explore her isolated wilderness, meet the Lozi people who live there, and learn how scientists and a community are bringing a once damaged ecosystem back to life.

Lady's story, like Liuwa's, is a story of death and rebirth, tragedy and hope, and having courage to continue when all seems lost. Today, right now, Liuwa's lions are being brought back from the edge of extinction. Through animal reintroduction, conservation, and research, an ecosystem is being restored. There is hope. These magical places can be saved—even those that are down to their last lioness.

—Bradley Hague, October 2015

Lady of Liuwa walks through camp at Liuwa Plain National Park.

Lady peers around a tree near
Matamanene Bush Camp.

CHAPTER 1

THE GREAT PLAINS

The Liuwa Plains, Zambia, Africa

WISDOM CAN COME FROM EVEN A SMALL ANTHILL.

—TONGA PROVERB

On first glance, the Liuwa Plains don't look like much. The land is flat and open. Scattered amid an almost endless expanse of tan grasses are small, dark green mounds of suffrutex plants that look like weeds. Islands of trees—some groupings just a few dozen feet across; others small forests the size of city blocks—are all that break the line of the horizon. The dome of the sky is massive. Underneath it, you feel exposed and small. But despite the somewhat empty feel, the Liuwa Plains are an incredible, complex, fascinating, and wonderful world.

Take those mounds of suffrutex, for example. From one angle, they appear small and weedlike, but they are really the highest leaves of hidden trees that grow from the top down and tap into water hidden underground. Those "tree islands" peeking above the parched landscape become literal islands for part of the year, when the plains transform into a massive shallow lake.

This is a land of stark contrasts and hidden wonders. There are two main seasons on the plains: dry and wet. During the height of the dry season, which begins in May and stretches through the end of September, temperatures can soar well over 100° F (38° C). The region practically bakes in the heat. The soil is a deep, fine sand, which makes walking, and even driving, difficult. Everything and everyone gets covered in a thin layer of dust. What little water

TOP: The Barotse royal barge, the Nalikwanda, leads the Kuomboka festival at the start of the rainy season.

BOTTOM: The red lechwe, a small antelope, thrives in the flooded marsh during Liuwa's wet season.

exists is trapped in rivers or in small shallow lakes, known as pans. The wet season starts in October, with the coming of the rains. The sky fills with towering clouds and lightning. As rain washes over the region, lush greenery and colorful flowers burst forth on the central plains, while the southern wetlands are buried underneath a lake that's up to three feet (0.9 m) deep.

Everything in the Liuwa Plains, from the mightiest lioness to the smallest snake and insect, lives by the cycle of these two seasons. When the rainy season starts, the humans abandon their villages, led by their kings and queens, in a ceremonial procession known as the Kuomboka; and the animals move to higher, drier grounds in the center of the park, where villages are forbidden.

Wildebeests and other herbivores leave their dry-season pastures near Zambia's northwestern border and swarm south in massive numbers to eat and enjoy the new grass. Their young come with them: wildebeest calves struggling on new legs; zebra colts under the eyes of their skittish parents. In the grasses, small antelope called oribis bound through as they are stalked by side-striped jackals and other mid-level hunters known as **mesopredators.** Cape buffalo graze at the edges of the Luanginga and Luambimba Rivers, where a few crocodiles wait in ambush.

Birds arrive as well. There are more than 300 different kinds of birds in Liuwa, and they come in every shape and size. There's the massive lappet-faced vulture, which has a nine-foot (2.7-m) wingspan and is the largest vulture in Africa. The saddle-billed stork is here, too. It stands taller than a man and needs a running start to fly into the air. Small kingfishers and plovers with bright wings and colorful crests

flit about in the trees. Wattled and crowned cranes mingle together in numbers found nowhere else on Earth.

At dawn and dusk, the top predators of the region can be found roaming the plains: hyena clans, packs of wild dogs, and even the occasional cheetah can be seen slinking, stalking, or sprinting after their prey. Hyenas are the top predator in the Liuwa Plains, with a population of about 500 animals spread out among numerous clans. Today, they are the undisputed king of the carnivores, but they are not the most famous. That honor belongs to the lions.

TOP: black crowned cranes in Liuwa Plain National Park
CENTER: Lightning strikes the Liuwa Plains during the summer storms.

hyenas in Liuwa Plain National Park

The golden grasses of the plains allow Liuwa's tawny lions to almost vanish into their environment.

THE LIONS OF LIUWA

The lions of Liuwa are perfectly suited to their environment. Their beige-colored coat is an ideal camouflage. Lions stalk within yards of their prey before pouncing in the tall, tan-colored grass. A lioness and even a male with a giant mane can blend in, seemingly invisible. Entire prides can hide in the grasses for carefully planned ambushes.

Lions' bodies are designed for hunting. They can reach speeds of up to 50 miles an hour (80 km/h) in a chase, and they can bring a 600-pound (272-kg) wildebeest crashing to the ground. Lions' size and power let them guard their hard-won kills from smaller scavengers. They use their retractable, razor-sharp claws to grip their prey and to tear open the carcass to eat.

Even lions' eyes are a wonder, bringing in ambient light from every source. This means lions can hunt at night using only starlight. During the day, their keen eyes can spot wildebeests and zebras from long distances.

Lions aren't always on the hunt though. If you want to find Lady and her pride, your best bet is to look in the shaded tree islands, where they like to nap. Lionesses sleep up to 18 hours a day, and males will occasionally sleep for more than 24 hours at a time. They'll hunt in the daytime if they're hungry or if prey comes foolishly close, but it's mostly at night that they prowl, patrol their territories, and search for food. There are few things more exciting than watching a lion pride head out into the night on a hunt.

Liuwa's lions are more than just amazing predators. They are what is known as a **keystone species.** Keystone species are animal groups that have a dramatic impact on their environment. Often they'll change the behaviors or actions of other animals in the environment, or even change the environment itself. Lions require a lot of land, space, and prey. Wherever lions are found in abundance, they are a sign of a healthy ecosystem.

TOP: Lions usually spend over half their time asleep.
BOTTOM: Even in lion-rich environments, the lionesses do most of the hunting.

A PRESERVE IS BORN

The Liuwa Plains are the crown jewel of the broader Barotse floodplains region—and have been for centuries, even before they became a national park. In the 1880s, this area was part of an independent kingdom called Barotseland. It was ruled by a king, whose name was Lubosi Lewanika I. Lewanika set aside the Liuwa Plains as a royal hunting preserve. All the land and animals in Liuwa belonged to the king, and only he could give permission to hunt there. He tasked the Lozi tribe with guarding and protecting the land. Their villages were placed on the edge of the preserve, where they have lived ever since.

The Lozi could use the land to grow crops, to graze cattle, and to fish. But hunting was governed by strict rules, and so were less obvious uses like harvesting wild grasses for mats and baskets and cutting poles for building houses. Even setting fires was restricted and ritualized.

The creation of the preserve was little noticed, but it marked a major turning point in African conservation history. This remote corner of an isolated kingdom became one of the oldest protected areas in all of Africa, and its protection endured well beyond the king's death.

Of course, the protection wasn't perfect. The king regularly granted hunting rights to his friends and patrons. Animals that were considered threatening, like lions, hippos, and crocodiles, were hunted out of fear or retaliation as well as enjoyment. The plains gained more complete protection when a large area was declared a national park in 1972, just eight years after Zambia gained independence from Britain. The rest of the king's land would be named as a game-management area, a place where people could live and hunt but would have to do so according to strict laws.

By then, the Lozi were just one more part of the ecosystem, which had stabilized around them.

RIGHT: Lubosi Lewanika I, the King of Barotseland

Lozi houses are well built on small hills to endure the storms and floods of the rainy season.

Liuwa Plain National Park is in far western Zambia. It is one of the most remote and least visited national parks in the country. Animals here often migrate to the northwest and into neighboring countries.

Mulonga

Luambimba

L i u w a

Liuwa Plain National Park

P l a i n

Rd. 459

Kuuli

Matamanene Bush Camp

Lone Palm

Munde

Sausage Tree

Chikaku

| 0 | 10 miles |
| 0 | 10 kilometers |

Entrance Gate

Luambimba

Luanginga

AFRICA

Indian Ocean

Atlantic Ocean

Liuwa Plain National Park (Park enlarged above)

ZAMBIA

| 0 | 1,000 miles |
| 0 | 1,000 kilometers |

Hyenas chase vultures away from a wildebeest kill.

HOW AN ECOSYSTEM WORKS

Each animal in an **ecosystem** like Liuwa's fills a special role, called a **niche.** These roles have slowly developed over millions of years into a particular set of skills and traits. The interaction of these animals and their roles creates a complex web across the ecosystem.

Scientists map these relationships to identify the role and place of an animal in an ecosystem. While it can be very hard to figure out exactly how animals interact, they can often be placed into different groups or levels based on what they eat.

When you organize them this way, the animals form a **trophic pyramid.** The decline of key species at the top or bottom of the pyramid can cause major disruptions to the entire system, and even cause the system to collapse entirely.

The rules and traditions that the king put in place for Liuwa softened the human impact on the ecosystem. Humans can really damage an ecosystem, but in this case they did not. The Lozi people changed the landscape, but not so much that they destroyed it. This stability sustained and supported the plains for centuries.

Unfortunately, that was about to change.

Lozi fishing camp

16

TROPHIC LAYERS

Mapping out how animals fit into an ecosystem is a difficult task.

Scientists group them in trophic layers, which show each animal's place within a food chain. Many animals are part of different food chains, and mapping all these food chains creates a food web, which shows animals' part in the broader ecosystem.

Primary producers are responsible for most of the nutrients in the ecosystem. These are grasses and other plants and form the base of a food chain.

Primary consumers are animals that eat primary producers. All herbivores, like wildebeests and water buffalo, fall into this category. Even oribis and small bugs are in this category.

Since predators get their energy from eating the animals that eat the grasses, they are called **secondary consumers.** A lizard, which eats bugs, or a wild dog, which eats wildebeests, both fall into this category.

Larger predators, like lions and hyenas, are **tertiary consumers.** They eat the things that eat others. Often these are the biggest animals in a system.

On average, it takes ten animals of a lower trophic level to support one animal in the trophic level above it. This is why there are always more herbivores than predators in an ecosystem. It is also what gives the food pyramid its shape.

TROPHIC PYRAMID

A trophic pyramid has primary producers, like grass, at the base. Above that are herbivores that eat the grasses. Secondary consumers are animals that eat the herbivores. At the top of the pyramid are large predators, like lions.

CHAPTER 2

THE DECLINE AND FALL OF THE LIUWA PLAINS

WHEN ELEPHANTS FIGHT, IT IS THE GRASS THAT SUFFERS.

—AFRICAN PROVERB

Lady and her lion siblings were born in a litter sometime around 2002. No one is quite sure how many siblings she may have had or even how many lions were left in the park or in the broader plains themselves. One thing was certain, most were dead. These small cubs were some of the last lions of the Liuwa Plains. The **apex predator,** the most powerful predator in the ecosystem, was down to its last litter.

As the 20th century drew to a close, the Liuwa Plains were radically changed from just a century before. The cultural traditions and isolation that had protected the lions' environment were stripped away. Their food chain was devastated. Poaching was common. Extinction seemed likely. In less than one generation of humans—the equivalent of four generations of lions—Liuwa's ecosystem had collapsed. It went from relatively stable to almost completely destroyed.

Why and how did this happen? What could cause such a dramatic change?

Nakawa, the lord of
Liuwa, wandering in
the Liuwa Plains

THE COLLAPSE OF GUARDIANSHIP

As the Lozi population grew, so did their effect on the environment. Tribal rules helped limit the damage, but they could do only so much.

In 1964, Zambia won its independence from Britain. What was a good thing to most of the country offered mixed blessings to the far-flung Liuwa Plains. The once independent kingdom of Barotseland, which included the Liuwa Plains, was absorbed into the new country. The local king was allowed to keep his throne but lost a lot of his powers. Traditional order began to fade. The Zambian government hired new gamekeepers as Liuwa's guardians.

As a result, the Lozi lost some of their ancient connection to the land and to the ecosystem. Deprived of their role as guardians, they began to lose their personal stake in maintaining Liuwa as it was. It seems like a minor change, swapping one group of protectors for another, but it wasn't.

The new gamekeepers weren't bad people, but because they came from other parts of the country, they didn't care about the land in the same way that the Lozi, who had lived off it for generations, did. In fact, the new gamekeepers didn't live there full-time, so the success of the park was less important to them. As a result, many of the new gamekeepers cut corners, turned a blind eye to bad behavior, and accepted bribes from hunters and poachers. It was the first chink in the armor that had protected the lions of Liuwa for so long.

an example of a typical poaching camp

a Lozi camp at sunset

TOP: Lozi fishermen sleep next to the river under nets to make sure they can start to fish at first light.
RIGHT: Wildebeests in the Liuwa Plains often compete with livestock for grazing land.

ANIMAL CONFLICT

Humans and animals don't often interact peacefully. It's hard to do so. Growing crops is difficult when wildebeests might move in and eat your garden. It's even harder to raise cattle in a region where there are few fences and lots of hungry predators. Every rustle of grass, every birdcall, could be the sign of a hidden predator. Just walking through the plains to fish for your family's dinner could be frightening.

As royal and cultural power weakened, more people acted on those fears. The result was more lions killed in snares or traps. Other threatening animals began to decline too: crocodiles, hippos, and even wild dogs.

Fire was another problem. Fire has always been a part of the Liuwa Plains. It destroys the tall grass, which leads to new plant life. Once the land is burned, new green shoots and grasses quickly bloom.

Fires like this one, started to burn out old grasses, can cause major problems in the Liuwa Plains.

For scientists, this is a measure of Liuwa's **ecological resilience**—its ability to bounce back from damage. The new grass is known as fire flush and is a reminder to many Lozi that growth can come from destruction.

But fire helps this ecosystem only in moderation. After the country's independence, as the power and authority of the king faded, the Lozi burned more of the grasses around their villages more often. They burned areas near their homes or fishing pans to prevent dangerous animals from hiding there. The Lozi used these cleared areas for farming, and they grazed their cattle on the nutrient-rich fire flush.

The Lozi didn't burn the grasses with the intention of harming the lions or the ecosystem. Life in Liuwa is hard for everyone. More farmland could mean healthier cattle, which could mean the difference between living well, scraping by, or starvation. Every year, the Lozi burned large areas of the plains, not knowing the extent of the damage they were doing.

That damage was about to get worse. The people of Zambia claimed their independence peacefully at the ballot box. Their neighbors in Angola, just west of Liuwa, weren't so fortunate. In 1975, civil war broke out in Angola, and the peace and protection of the nearby Liuwa Plains was shattered.

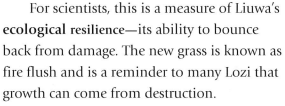

TOP: The Lozi are careful to protect cattle from predators.

WAR COMES TO LIUWA

The civil war in Angola raged for almost three decades and didn't always stay inside the country. Throughout the war, armies moved back and forth across the Angolan-Zambian border and into the Liuwa Plains. Suddenly, huge numbers of hungry soldiers with guns came into Liuwa, and there was little to stop them. Soldiers lived for years by eating and selling wildebeests. As resources became scarce and starvation became a real risk, the local people also started poaching for food. Previously, Lozi hunting had been limited and small scale. During the war, poaching was common and the impact was overwhelming.

Even before the war, the number of wildebeests in the Liuwa Plains was falling. At its height, Liuwa supported more than 100,000 wildebeests. By the time the war was over, there were just over 10,000 wildebeests left. In a mere 25 years, almost 90 percent of the wildebeests had been killed.

The zebra population was cut in half, and tsessebes (SEH-se-bees)—large antelope with the size and bulk of a cow—were completely driven off. The eland, another large antelope that was a symbol of the Lozi tribe, and the iconic Cape buffalo both went **locally extinct,** which means they were totally gone from the region. Hippos and elephants were eliminated as well. Near the rivers in the wetlands, the crocodile population plummeted. The adult crocodiles were killed because they were considered threatening, and their eggs were gathered for food. Every animal suffered.

elephant tusks, rhino horns, and other trophies seized from poachers in Zambia

24

Government soldiers stand by a truck full of weapons seized in the Angolan civil war.

No ecosystem could handle such a loss. The wildebeest herds were vital to supporting Liuwa's large population of carnivores: the lions, hyenas, cheetahs, and wild dogs. Now all the carnivores suddenly had to fight over one-tenth the amount of food. The famed predators of Liuwa, including the legendary lions, were on the verge of starvation. Unfortunately, this bad situation only got worse as a new threat entered the picture.

As the war in Angola dragged on, trophy hunters moved in, taking advantage of the chaos and weak rules in the park. Unlike the soldiers, who hunted for food, the trophy hunters took aim at the top of the ecosystem. Cheetahs were killed for their pelts, wild dogs were killed for sport, and at the top of the list, the mighty lions were killed for their manes, their meat, and the hunter's ego.

The damage was horrific. During the mid-1990s these majestic animals, the keystones of the ecosystem, were slaughtered. The cheetah population was driven locally extinct. Wild dogs completely disappeared.

Under the unrelenting guns, traps, and snares of poachers, the Liuwa ecosystem fell apart.

THE LEGEND OF THE SOLE SURVIVOR

In 2003, peace finally settled over the Angola-Zambia border, and people began to visit the area again. Rumors spread about a lone lioness that still lived in Liuwa. Though she was rarely seen and easily scared away, in 2004 a filmmaker named Herbert Brauer finally caught her on camera. Despite the devastation, despite the poachers, despite the odds, there was indeed one last lion in Liuwa.

She appeared to be in wonderful health, sleek and strong. Her only flaw was a scar that ran across her nose. Her discovery and her story brought new attention to Liuwa, both for the damage it had suffered and for the amazing wilderness it still was. The story of the last lioness would change everything.

Lady of Liuwa rests in grass.

When Lady was first photographed in 2004, she seemed like just another animal. Herbert Brauer continued to film her, and as Lady began to follow him and his crew around, she seemingly grew comfortable with them.

One day she came up to their car and rolled on her back, purring like a kitten. When lions do this, it is a sign of playfulness and friendliness. This is almost never done for humans. So, it was a shock to the team—and a sign of just how lonely Lady was.

Lady even followed the crew back to their camp. The crew was terrified of her reaction, but she simply flopped down on the ground and purred. She did this routinely, over the next few weeks, seemingly searching for some form of company.

But Lady wasn't after human companionship. Her calls and cries were designed for other lions, and there were none around. Humans were the closest things to friends and family she had. Brauer's film, called *The Last Lioness,* made Lady famous around the world, and the film crew was there to watch as Lady's loneliness ended and her small pride was formed.

Lady playfully rolls for the cameras.

Herbert Brauer with Lady in Liuwa Plain National Park

CHAPTER 3

A LIUWA WITHOUT LIONS

THE USEFULNESS OF
A WELL IS KNOWN WHEN
IT DRIES UP.

—AFRICAN PROVERB

Animals don't just live in their environments; they shape them, too. In North America, beavers build dams that create lakes where other animals eat and drink. In African jungles, elephants stomp out paths that other species use as roads to move about the forest. Even small behaviors can have significant impacts.

Lions sleep in the shade of the tree islands, sheltered from the hot sun. When hunting, the lions seek out the tall grass, which hides them from their prey. Wildebeests avoid these areas, remaining in places with short grass where they can see lions and other threats coming. Zebras use herds of wildebeests as cover, since predators often go after them first. Wildebeests use zebras as lookouts since they are more alert and likely to see predators. Over the years these behaviors and patterns can reshape an ecosystem as dramatically as a beaver dam or an elephant trail.

The hunting and poaching of Liuwa's top predators was the environmental equivalent of tearing down a dam or blowing up a road. The damage it caused had the potential to destabilize the entire area. When an apex

Without the presence of lions, hyenas became the top predators in the Liuwa Plains.

TOP: Lady of Liuwa
CENTER: A wildebeest faces off
with a wild dog pack in Liuwa.

predator disappears, it causes something called a **trophic cascade.** During a trophic cascade, the entire order of the ecosystem is upended, and changes ripple throughout the region, affecting the behavior of almost every animal in it.

A new balance had to be found. New animal behaviors emerged, forming new risks and dangers.

Hyenas and side-striped jackals typically scavenge from lions but are also hunted by them. Lions often attack hyenas on sight and can easily kill them. Without lions, Liuwa's hyena population grew unchecked and led to new risks for the ecosystem. The lions had helped keep the largest herbivores, like the buffalo and zebras, in check. If the system was left alone too long, the zebra and buffalo populations could grow and graze without much fear. Although this wasn't an immediate danger, since poaching had diminished those populations so much, it was still a threat to the long-term success of the system.

Scientists began to follow Lady and track her using a satellite collar to learn how she managed life on her own. As long as Lady lived, the lions of Liuwa weren't extinct, though they were terrifyingly close. To survive, Lady needed to learn to hunt alone. She had to stalk closer, sprint faster, and go farther than most lionesses. If she was spotted by her prey too soon, the hunt would be over, and she

Lions often chase
and even kill hyenas
to defend their food.

TOP: Zebras herd together on the Liuwa Plains.
RIGHT: Hartebeest herds run across the Liuwa Plains.

would go hungry. Patience became key and strategy was vital.

She also needed to learn when to fight and when not to fight. Hyenas will not pick on a pride of lions at a kill. Alone, however, Lady and her kills were easy targets. Without backup, Lady was forced to choose between giving up her meals or fighting and potentially giving up her life. Often, she went hungry.

With Lady and prides of lions no longer able to fulfill the role as the ecosystem's apex predator, the hyenas stepped in to fill the gap. The hyenas did not rise to power out of hatred or envy—animals do not operate like that. Without lion kills to scavenge from, hyenas had to hunt more of their own prey. And without lions to be afraid of, hyenas could thrive like never before.

Scientists call this **competitive release** since hyenas were "released" from competition with the lions for food. Without that competition, the hyena population grew and expanded its territory like never before. What is good for hyenas and wild dogs, though, is bad for the things they hunt. Zebras thrive in the absence of lions, their main predator, but wildebeests still had to fear roaming clans of hyenas. Hyenas may also hunt lizards, oribis, and other prey that lions would ignore. As the threat of lions disappeared, the Liuwa Plains became dominated by clans of hyenas.

Wildebeest herds can number in the hundreds and even thousands as they move through the plains.

THE RESTORATION BEGINS

The devastation of the Angolan civil war was broadcast in Zambia and the wider world. But the ecological cost was less well known. The discovery of Lady, the sole lion survivor, sparked an international interest in the Liuwa Plains. People understood that Liuwa was a precious land, and its previous protections should be restored.

In 2002, the Angolan civil war ended. The next year, the government of Zambia teamed up with the Barotse royal government and a private group called African Parks to manage the Liuwa Plain National Park. African Parks would get to run and manage the national park, but it would also have to try to rebuild the broader Liuwa Plains ecosystem. This led to a major, almost unanswerable question: How do you actually restore an ecosystem, and how do you know when you have done it?

Ecosystems are incredibly intricate and interconnected. Every piece is important and whole chunks of this ecosystem had been destroyed. Liuwa may have been protected for over a century, but it had not been intensely studied. No one really knew how many different types and numbers of animals lived there in the past or exactly how many had to be replaced to restore Liuwa. How could they rebuild it if they did not even know what they had lost?

THE ANIMAL SYSTEMS

Lions can jump as far as 36 feet (11 m) in a chase.

To restore the ecosystem, researchers had to focus not on rebuilding animal numbers but on re-creating all the systems within the plains. That way, the animals could appropriately impact the environment. An ecosystem can have many configurations, but some pieces are always required. Several things happen only when animals reach large enough numbers to contribute to a healthy system. Among these are **predation,** when animals hunt all their typical prey; **migration,** when animals move from place to place in search of food; **competition,** when different species compete with one another for territory or food; reproduction, when animals successfully raise offspring to adulthood; and **dispersion,** when animals move away into new areas and expand their range.

Scientists measure the interaction of these elements to determine an animal's **ecological effectiveness,** or its influence on the system. A good ecosystem has all of the animals in it, functioning in the system effectively.

Of course, the last lioness was unable to fully take part in this system. Lady lived on a diet of wildebeests alone because she was unable to hunt the faster, more alert zebras without help. Zebras are more dangerous and fight back, and Lady couldn't risk the chance of injury. Her lonely existence meant competition with the hyenas was impossible. Reproduction

and dispersion required finding a mate, so they were out, too.

Lady was not the only animal in this predicament. Few animal species in the Liuwa ecosystem truly lived their roles. The migration routes of the remaining wildebeests shrank dramatically. A small herd does not require a large amount of space, so the area they needed to graze was smaller than it had ever been. They still left the plains in the dry season, but their epic historical migration was greatly reduced. As for competition, the main animal numerous enough to guard and battle over territory was the newly crowned apex predator, the hyena.

When the conflict in Angola ended, Liuwa was a shadow of its former glory, but there was still hope. Some believed that the animals of the plains could rebound, much like those bright green shoots of fire flush grow in the aftermath of a blaze. An ecosystem this complex was going to take time, effort, and dedication to restore.

It was not going to be a quick task.

LEFT: Wildebeest calves travel south to eat the new grass in Liuwa.

Researchers spend long lonely hours tracking animals through the plains.

TRACKING ANIMALS

Scientists are often able to predict animals' locations based on their understanding of animal behavior. Several tools make it easier for scientists to track the animals' movements.

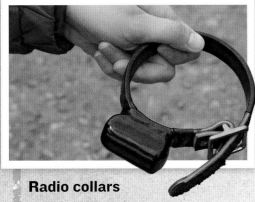

Radio collars

These collars emit low-powered beeps that can be picked up on a handheld antenna. The collars have a limited range but can lead trackers straight to the animal. Radio collars can last for two to three years before they need to be replaced.

Satellite collars

Satellite collars use GPS to beam the exact location of the animal to a computer every few hours year-round. Satellite collars provide more data but are more expensive and do not last as long as radio collars. Lady and Sepo both have satellite collars to track their exact location around the clock.

GPS tracking

Maps are key to understanding an ecosystem over time. By locating water sources, plants, tree islands, and other physical features of the park, with radio and satellite tags, scientists can learn details about animal habits even when the animals are never seen.

Rangers mark important sites into a handheld GPS.

Sepo, wearing a satellite collar, drinks from a watering hole.

CHAPTER 4

HOW TO BUILD AN ECOSYSTEM

TO GET LOST IS TO LEARN THE WAY.

—AFRICAN PROVERB

As the new management took over Liuwa Plain National Park, local scouts, guides, and guards began to search for poachers and to protect the wildlife once again. The response was immediate and profound. As the pressure from poaching dropped, the animal populations soared. Wildebeest herds grew immediately, adding hundreds and then thousands of animals a year. Zebras, tsessebes, and oribis came back. Wild dogs and cheetahs, which had been thought extinct, suddenly made a return to the plains. In 2008, even a few elephants wandered into the park, though they quickly left as well. None of these animals were back in great numbers, but their return was a good sign.

Unfortunately, it was only a partial recovery, as important pieces of the system were still missing. The buffalo were gone, as were the eland, and Lady remained the only lion. The animal population in Liuwa could grow significantly, but those species that were lost could never be replaced. Without them, the system would be unstable, or at least incomplete. These animals had served important functions. The plains needed them. If Liuwa was going to have the buffalo and eland it once did, if Lady was not going to be its last lioness, then new animals would have to be brought in to fill the void.

A scout uses a radio tracker to monitor wildebeests in the park.

REINTRODUCTIONS

eland

Animal reintroductions, or bringing new animals into an area where others of their kind once roamed, are complicated, costly, and extremely risky. To even consider them means that the whole region is out of balance. There is no hope that the needed animals would migrate or disperse into Liuwa on their own. It is a desperation move, a last resort. Still, sometimes even desperate moves are successful.

With studied care, the scientists and managers at Liuwa set about assembling the list of animals that would need to be reintroduced. Finding a mate for Lady was a priority, but far from the only one. The Cape buffalo, one of the most well-known herbivores in Africa and a vital food source for lions, was another priority, as was the eland. For centuries the eland had been one of the cultural symbols of the Lozi, and its restoration would help reestablish those ancient connections.

While necessary to restore the ecosystem, the reintroductions weren't always popular. The Lozi make their living farming and herding. Large herbivores like the tsessebe, buffalo, and eland can trample fences and eat domestic gardens. They also graze on the same lands as the Lozi's cattle. Not everyone was sad to see the animals go, and not everyone wanted them back.

Nonetheless, in 2007, a new herd of 49 eland was added to the park and began to weave itself back into the ecosystem. Their numbers and ecological impact were small, but it meant the recovery was under way. The next year, 16 buffalo were brought from other parks and placed in the Liuwa Plains. Some were

Scouts use motorcycles and radio trackers to help defend wildlife in Liuwa.

given tracking collars so scientists could follow their movements. In the beginning, the buffalo herd was so small that it could not defend itself. Scouts and managers had to spend their days riding motorcycles with the herd to drive away predators until the herd could increase their number and ability to defend themselves.

The new additions were small, but they started to grow quickly. The ecosystem grew and adapted to the new, more peaceful order.

For the ecosystem to be truly restored, though, the predators of the eland and buffalo also needed to be reintroduced. This was a major problem: If adding herbivores back to the Liuwa Plains was controversial and scary to the locals, that was even truer of bringing in the lions.

REBUILDING THE PRIDE

Lions at a zoo can look quiet and cuddly, but a hungry lion is a powerful, fierce beast. In addition, the Lozi, like many other cultures, highly value their cattle. Across Africa, the conflict between lions and humans over cattle causes tragedy. The more lions that came to Liuwa, the more the Lozi cattle would be at risk. However, lions also bring tourists and money. As word spread about Lady, so did her global popularity. For a time, she became the most famous lion in the world. People wanted to see her and to see her become part of a new pride. If Liuwa could bring in more tourists, the money could help support the Lozi. An intense debate ensued among the local people, the scientists, and the conservationists protecting Liuwa.

What may have swayed the debate was Lady herself. Despite her many years hunting in the area, Lady had never shown any interest in the Lozi livestock. She stayed away from the villages, the humans, and their cattle. Her diet was mostly wildebeest, with the occasional zebra calf or anything else she could scrounge for good measure. Some thought Lady would raise her cubs to hunt in the same way, which would be the best of all possible options. The Lozi would get the benefits of the lions without much risk to their cattle. It took a lot of persuading, but eventually everyone agreed. Lions would return to Liuwa.

Oribi

wildebeest

However, this was easier said than done.

In addition to their many other talents, lions have a very strong homing instinct, which means they try to find their way back home. If you picked up a lion from the other side of Zambia and dropped it in the Liuwa Plains, it's not likely to just stay there. It'll try to head back to its original home. This endangers not only the lion but also the villagers and cattle along the route. A lion that tries to make that journey would likely be killed.

To stop the lions from leaving Liuwa, the scientists set up a place called a *boma*, which means "fence" or "enclosure," in one of the tree islands. The hope was that after a few weeks, they would adapt to life in Liuwa and would not want to leave. However, most lions travel hundreds of miles in a week and have never seen a fence. They do not like being trapped, even in what we would call a large area. They roar, attack the fence, and try to escape. Still, the boma is necessary to protect them until they can be freed.

Scientists also had to identify a good match to be Lady's mate. They selected a lion from Zambia's Kafue National Park, over 250 miles (400 km) away. Scientists hoped that once the male lion adapted to his new surroundings and was introduced to Lady, the two would start a family, and the population of lions would increase throughout the generations.

The transfer of the new lion seemed to go smoothly. But tragedy struck as the new lord of Liuwa was recovering from his journey: He choked while eating a wildebeest, which had been left for him, and he died the first night he was in the park. Lady never even saw him.

Intimidated but determined, scientists made a second attempt in 2009. This time, they brought two males to Liuwa. Tracking collars were placed on both of them so that their movements could be monitored. This

Lions linger at the edge of a wildebeest herd.

Nakawa and Sepo, the parents of Liuwa's cubs

second attempt also seemed to go well. The lions arrived, arose, and began to explore their new surroundings, roaring, pacing, and marking their new territory.

To everyone's amazement and excitement, Lady responded. From then on, Lady was never far from the lion boma. Though she was separated from them by a fence, there were at last other lions in Liuwa. Lady was not alone.

Every day, scientists, scouts, and a crew of filmmakers came to the fence to follow the lions, but then panic struck. On the fifth day, as they drove up to the enclosure, they saw that a section of the fence had collapsed. The lions had escaped, and Lady was nowhere to be found! Given the lion's homing instinct, the scientists feared the worst: that the lions had left Liuwa to travel the hundreds of miles back to Kafue National Park. On the edge of success, the scientists worried that they had lost the lions again.

Thankfully, as the scientists searched for Lady, using her tracking collar, they found her curled up in the shade under the trees, the two males sleeping beside her. The new pride was nearly inseparable. Over the next few months, the lions mated, and it seemed like it would be only a matter of time before lion cubs once again scampered across the plains.

Scientists watched with cautious optimism. Lady was an old lioness, and they were not sure if she was past the point at which she could have cubs of her own. As the months ticked by without Lady becoming pregnant, those fears were confirmed. But by now, the conservation team had come too far to give up. So, in 2011, they went back to Kafue National Park and brought two new female lions to the Liuwa pride. The new females were young and did not always seem to enjoy Lady's company, but for the most part, they seemed to get along. The two males and two females offered new hope to the plains and ended Lady's years of loneliness.

At last, after almost ten years alone for Lady, and a year's worth of false starts and bad luck for the scientists, Lady lived again with lions. There was a functioning pride once again.

Lady and her new pride relax in the Liuwa Plains.

ANIMAL RELOCATION

Animal relocation requires months of planning, timing, and preparation. It can be broken down into four steps:

Planning

Young lions are identified in nearby parks where they can be safely extracted. Animals are chosen based on age, genetics, and behavior. Wild lions are preferred because their instincts and genetic diversity remain intact. Once the lions are selected, all the logistics are arranged, including trucks to carry the animals, vets to tranquilize and care for them, and filing of permits.

Capture

Trackers and spotters will follow the lions until they reach a safe place. Specially trained wildlife vets tranquilize the lions, and as soon as the lions are unconscious, the team swoops into action. They make sure the lions are still safe to transport, move them into cages, and place them onto trucks. The vets then ride along with the lions, keeping them safe and sedated for the often hours-long trip to their new home.

Adaptation

Once in their new park, the animals are released from the cages and placed in a boma, or enclosure, to prevent the animals from returning to their original park, and they are given food to help them adapt. They may also be given tracking collars to allow scientists to keep watch over them.

Release

After a few days or weeks, the doors of the boma are opened, and the animals can wander into their new home.

CHAPTER 5

THE LIUWA PLAINS TODAY

**THE BEST TIME TO PLANT
A TREE IS 20 YEARS AGO;
THE SECOND-BEST TIME IS NOW.**

—ANCIENT PROVERB

Almost every night, just after dusk, the lions of Liuwa begin their prowl, slinking through the growing darkness. For much of the year, rain or shine, hot or cold, the lions have company. A team of scientists from the Zambian Carnivore Programme follows them. The scientists never help, they never interfere, but they are the eyes and ears monitoring Liuwa's progress. They are the witnesses to Liuwa's slow rebirth.

The hunts can go on all night, and the next day there's more work for the scientists to do. They follow the wildebeests and the zebras, generating census counts and trying to figure out what impact the animals are having on Liuwa's changing landscape. They track the animals using satellite and radio collars to follow their migrations in and around the park. They also collect samples of what the animals eat and what they leave behind.

Park rangers, animal conservationists, and scientists all are hard at work to conserve, restore, and research the Liuwa Plains.

The work is vital to understanding how the ecosystem is changing as it heals and whether the experiment is a success.

The scientists live year-round at the remote Matamanene Bush Camp, which is set amid a tree island. They share the camp with scouts and anti-poaching patrols dedicated to keeping the animals safe. The dangers are still great, and tragedies have struck time and again.

Of the adult lions that were brought from Kafue National Park to live in the Liuwa Plains, only two remain. Just eight months after the young female lions were reintroduced in 2011, one of them was caught in a poacher's snare and killed. Liuwa's scientists, trackers, and protectors are constantly on the lookout for snares and traps, but these are still being set, and the protectors cannot eliminate them all.

In June 2012, the surviving female left the park, seemingly headed toward Angola. The scientists scrambled to catch up to her. They just barely made it. She was tranquilized, captured, and brought back to Liuwa. Lions don't recognize human borders, whether of a park or a country, and outside of the Liuwa Plains, lions are frighteningly at risk.

In fall 2013, the two males of Lady's pride crossed over into Angola and out of the protection of the national park. When the lions were in Angola, they encountered a local village. Confused and afraid for their lives, the villagers killed the younger lion. Its elder brother escaped and headed back to safety: to Liuwa. If he had encountered any other villagers, poachers, or snares, the entire restoration effort could have been doomed. Thankfully, he made it. The male lion's return led the small pride, now only three lions strong, to become even closer, and in 2014 there was reason to celebrate. Cubs were born! For possibly the first time since Lady herself was young, the playful yips and growls of lion cubs could be heard on the Liuwa Plains. Lady now looked over a new generation of three

Lady of Liuwa

energetic cubs. As part of the excitement, the lion parents were given new names. The father of the cubs became Nakawa, which means "he who gives back" in the Lozi language. The mother is called Sepo, which means "hope." The birth of the cubs was greeted with joy around the world. Lady would not be the last lioness of Liuwa.

The restoration seemed well on the road to success when yet another disaster struck. Scientists noticed that Nakawa's tracking collar had stopped moving. Lions may like their sleep, but they rarely stay stationary for too long; a stationary tracker is almost always a bad sign. When the scientists got to the tracked location, their worst fears were confirmed. Nakawa was found dead inside the park, seemingly poisoned.

Despite this loss, Lady, Sepo, and the cubs grow bold and brave, and the pride hunts more often. The lions are slowly becoming a threat to Liuwa's zebras and other herbivores once again.

Today, the wildebeest herds are growing rapidly and beginning to return to

LEFT: A cub sharpens its claws on a tree.
BOTTOM: Researchers use radio tracking to help tourists find animals at Liuwa Plain National Park.

Sepo lies with two of her three cubs at Liuwa Plain National Park.

their ancient migration. Despite the wildebeest decline during the Angolan war, this migration is still the second largest wildebeest migration in the world, and an awe-inspiring sight for tourists, scientists, and locals alike.

Zebras have doubled in population and now have to keep ever more alert as the lions have reemerged as a threat to their survival. The buffalo, Liuwa's largest herbivores, which were once completely extinct, are now almost 100 strong. Today, they can protect themselves and have begun to reestablish their role in the ecosystem. Eland, the symbol of the Lozi, are back as well.

Migration, predation, competition, reproduction—slowly, the systems that kept the plains stable for so long are coming back. The ecosystem of the Liuwa Plains is still damaged, and the snares of poachers are a real threat, but the ancient connections between the animals and the people are returning, too.

The hyenas remain the top predator in Liuwa, in terms of population and kills, but their days are numbered. It will be many years, even decades, before lions regain their place as the undisputed top predators in Liuwa. But life for the hyenas will only get harder.

Stealing from the pride has become more difficult, now that other lions can guard the kill. Even the wild dogs are coming back, with new packs and dens showing up every year. As these predators thrive, the hyena will diminish and return to their traditional role as hunters and scavengers.

The wildebeest population has grown rapidly, though its odds of living and thriving get worse as the predators return. Less than half the calves born in a year will survive to adulthood, and that number is falling. This,

A flock of birds, including sacred ibises and spoonbills, take flight over Liuwa.

too, is part of the natural order, and a sign the ecosystem is coming back.

This restoration affects the entire animal world and the humans who live within it. Today, for the Lozi, the animals of Liuwa are more than just nuisances or threats. They are potential opportunities, gateways to education, employment, and a better life. By taking care of the ecosystem and protecting the lions, the Lozi are taking care of themselves. As more guards, guides, and scouts reestablish their cultural connection to the plains, the number of tourists increases.

Lions lurking in the grass are still terrifying, but they now bring tourists, money, and jobs, which help support the Lozi who protect them. The amazing animals, beautiful birds, lush landscape, and, of course, Lady, now inspire travelers from all over the world.

More than 100 years ago, the ruler of Barotseland, Lubosi Lewanika I, created Liuwa as a protected wilderness. Today it is protected again, but for the good of all. This vast, beautiful, seemingly endless wilderness teaches us how fragile even remote ecosystems are, and how complicated it can be to rebuild them, but also why it is worth doing so.

Liuwa is now making history through conservation. And, like the bright green fire flush that arises in the wake of destruction, it is blooming once more.

REINTRODUCING ANIMALS

Animal reintroductions aren't limited to Africa. Yellowstone National Park in Wyoming, U.S.A., is another ecosystem that is being restored.

The top predator in Yellowstone, the gray wolf, had been hunted to extinction for almost a century, and the ecosystem was thrown badly off balance. Elk were allowed to grow unchecked and overgrazed the young trees, hurting other animals. Large herds also spread diseases and sickness around the park. Human hunters were used for many years to keep the elk population in check. Coyotes stepped into the apex predator role, causing other problems.

In 1995, wolves were reintroduced to the area as a natural check on the elk. The reintroduction started small, but 20 years later, the results are extraordinary. Today, almost 100 gray wolves roam Yellowstone. They are an ecologically effective force once again. Elk numbers have dropped, and the survivors are healthier and less damaging to the landscape.

Beaver, fox, and rabbit populations have also increased as the elk have stopped overgrazing. The ecosystem is healing and stabilizing. The reintroductions caused bigger changes and were more successful than scientists had ever anticipated.

RIGHT: gray wolf
BOTTOM: elk in Yellowstone

Nakawa and his
brother in the
Liuwa Plains

Liuwa Restored

Every year, as the rains race across the horizon, wildebeests make their way south. They come in the thousands, in massive herds that blacken the horizon. The young calves are with them, slowly learning the routines and realities of life in the Liuwa Plains. Zebras, tsessebes, and eland are scattered among them, too. Waiting in the tall grass, the lions of Liuwa watch.

In the night, the yips of hyenas and roars of lions echo in the darkness. The hyenas, once the dominant predators in the whole ecosystem, now keep an eye out for the lions and wild dogs as well as for the wildebeests. Their place as Liuwa's premier predator is no longer secure.

In the sky and on the ground, birds are everywhere. Massive wading birds like the crowned crane and saddle-billed stork linger near the pans. Huge birds of prey, like the African fish eagle and the lappet-faced vulture, soar overhead.

The Liuwa Plains was once a protected place where the local people lived and worked as part of an ecosystem that supported them. It can be that again.

It will take luck, effort, and research to get there. There are still threats to Liuwa from poachers who hunt lions for their body parts or hunt wildebeests for meat. Despite these risks, the system is slowly coming back.

A restored Liuwa is not a paradise. There is always a risk of civil instability. And there will always be human-animal conflict, as there has been since the first humans came to the plains. Still, Liuwa can thrive.

By rebuilding the animal systems that form the heart of a functioning ecosystem, the Liuwa Plains can find balance in a way that supports humans as well as wildlife. It can bring together the people who live there, the animals who call the land home, and the tourists who dream of seeing an astonishing African wilderness.

It can also be an example. Across the world, there are places that have been damaged by human actions and places where animals have been driven to extinction or reduced to the edge of oblivion. These, too, can be restored.

At the turn of the new millennium, the Liuwa Plains was a dying land. Its cheetah had disappeared, its wild dogs were gone, and it was down to its last lion. Today scientists, park managers, and people of the Liuwa Plains are showing that, through patience, integrity, effort, and science, the animals and the environment can be restored.

Wild dogs have returned to Liuwa.

ANIMALS OF THE LIUWA PLAINS

Thousands of animals, from small insects and snakes to massive lions and buffalo, live on the Liuwa Plains. Here are some examples.

PREDATORS
(animals that hunt other animals for food)

AFRICAN LION
The lion is the only social cat in Liuwa. It lives in family-based prides, mostly on plains and grasslands.

AFRICAN WILD DOG
Different from domesticated dogs, the African wild dog hunts in packs ranging from 6 to 20 dogs strong. It often hunts wildebeests and other large herbivores.

CHEETAH
The cheetah usually lives and hunts alone or in pairs. Its meals often get stolen by other hungry predators.

SIDE-STRIPED JACKAL
One of the meso-predators of the plains, the side-striped jackal often hunts small animals or scavenges off other animals' kills.

SPOTTED HYENA
The most numerous and successful social carnivore on the plains, the spotted hyena lives in family clans. Liuwa's hyenas hunt more than they scavenge and form close-knit family groups.

HERBIVORES
(animals that eat only plants)

CAPE BUFFALO
Weighing up to 600 pounds (272 kg), the African Cape buffalo is hunted almost solely by lions and people. Its fused horns form a shield, called a boss.

ELAND
The symbol of the Lozi for centuries, the eland is a large member of the antelope family. It is about the size of a horse and has spiral-shaped horns.

HARTEBEEST
As a member of the antelope family, the hartebeest feeds on grasslands and moves in herds of up to 300. It has long, curved horns, which are often used for sparring over territory.

ORIBI
This diminutive antelope grows to only about two feet (0.6 m) high and is commonly seen grazing in the short grasses.

TSESSEBE
Another antelope variant, the tsessebe is a large cattle-like animal with spiral horns and a distinctive hump on its back.

WILDEBEEST
Also known as gnu, the wildebeest is a member of the antelope family and is one of the most easily spotted animals in Liuwa.

ZEBRA
The skittish zebra is the most easily identifiable animal on the plains. Scientists still debate the reason for their stripes, but agree that every zebra pattern is unique.

GLOSSARY

apex predator: The most powerful predator in an ecosystem

competition: The struggle between different species for territory or food

competitive release: An increase in the number of one species after a separate species it competes with is eliminated

dispersion: The act of animals moving into new areas outside their normal habitat

ecological effectiveness: When an animal or another organism is carrying out its proper role in an ecosystem

ecological resilience: A measure of an ecosystem's ability to adapt to and bounce back from damage

ecosystem: A geographic area where plants, animals, and other organisms interact with the landscape. Ecosystems are shaped by both their geography and the animals and organisms that inhabit them.

keystone species: Animal groups that have a dramatic impact on their environment despite their small number

locally extinct: The complete elimination of an animal species from a certain area; also called extirpation. This is different from a globalized extinction, in which no individual animals of a species exist at all.

mesopredator: A smaller predator that hunts for food but is itself hunted or threatened by other predators

migration: Repeated movement of animals from one place to another for food, weather, or safety

niche: The basic role and position an animal occupies in the environment; also known as ecological role

predation: The act of hunting

predators: Animals that kill and eat other animals to survive

trophic cascade: A disruption in a food chain in which the animals at the very top are eliminated, causing problems for animals farther down on the food chain

trophic layer: A way of categorizing animals according to what they eat. Trophic layers make up the trophic pyramid and are often used in mapping food chains and food webs.

trophic pyramid: A system categorizing animals according to where they are in relation to what they eat and what eats them.

kingfisher

INDEX

PHOTO CREDITS

Cover (CTR), Stephen Cunliffe; Back Cover (CTR), Stephen Cunliffe; (UP RT), Stephen Cunliffe; (UP CTR), Stephen Cunliffe; (UP LE), Lorenz Andreas Fischer; Front Flap (LO), Lorenz Andreas Fischer; Spine (UP), Stephen Cunliffe; Back Flap, Bradley Hague; 1 (CTR), Michelle Attala; 2 (CTR), Lorenz Andreas Fischer; 4 (CTR), Dale Morris; 6 (LO), Lorenz Andreas Fischer; 7 (CTR), Stephen Cunliffe; 8 (CTR), Lorenz Andreas Fischer; 10 (LE), Hemis/Alamy; 10 (CTR), Lorenz Andreas Fischer; 11 (UP), Lorenz Andreas Fischer; 11 (CTR), Lorenz Andreas Fischer; 11 (LO), Lorenz Andreas Fischer; 12 (CTR), Stephen Cunliffe; 13 (UP), Sérgio Nogueira/Dreamstime; 13 (LO), Anup Shah/Nature Picture Library; 14 (UP), Hulton-Deutsch Collection/Corbis; 14 (LO), Michelle Attala; 16 (UP), Lorenz Andreas Fischer; 16 (LO), Michelle Attala; 17 (UP), Egil Droge/Zambian Carnivore Programme; 17 (UP CTR), Lorenz Andreas Fischer; 17 (LO CTR), Lorenz Andreas Fischer; 17 (LO), enciktat/Shutterstock; 18 (CTR), Stephen Cunliffe; 20 (LO), Lorenz Andreas Fischer; 20 (UP), Egil Droge/Zambian Carnivore Programme; 21 (UP), Michelle Attala; 21 (LO), Stephen Cunliffe; 22 (CTR), Michelle Attala; 23 (UP), Paul Godard; 24 (LE), Sue Cunningham Photographic/Alamy; 25 (CTR), Scott Peterson/Liaison/Getty Images; 26 (LO LE), Lorenz Andreas Fischer; 26 (UP CTR), Bryan Busovicki/Dreamstime; 26, Lorenz Andreas Fischer; 26 (LO), Paul Godard; 27 (LO), Fergus Clark/Aquavision TV Productions; 27 (UP), Paul Godard; 28 (CTR), Lorenz Andreas Fischer; 30 (UP), Paul Godard; 30 (CTR), Stephen Cunliffe; 30 (LO), Anup Shah/Nature Picture Library; 31 (UP), Dale Morris; 31 (CTR), Dale Morris; 32 (UP), Anup Shah/Minden Pictures; 33 (LO), Denis-Huot/Minden Pictures; 34 (UP), Lorenz Andreas Fischer; 34 (LO), Paul Godard; 35 (UP), John Eveson/FLPA/Minden Pictures; 35 (CTR), Roland Seitre/Nature Picture Library; 35 (LO), Paul Godard; 36-37 (CTR), Paul Godard; 38 (RT), Nico Smit/Dreamstime; 39 (LE), Dale Morris; 39 (CTR), Lorenz Andreas Fischer; 39 (RT), Lorenz Andreas Fischer; 39 (LO), iStockphoto; 40 (UP), Pal Teravagimov/Shutterstock; 40 (LO), Stephen Cunliffe; 41 (CTR), Paul Godard; 42 (UP), Dale Morris; 42 (LO), Paul Godard; 43 (LO), Daniel Born/The Times/Gallo Images/Getty Images; 43 (CTR), Themba Hadebe/AP Photo; 43 (UP), Malcolm Schuyl/Minden Pictures; 44 (CTR), Egil Droge/Zambian Carnivore Programme; 44 (UP), Paul Godard; 46 (RT), Stephen Cunliffe; 46 (LO), Egil Droge/Zambian Carnivore Programme; 46 (CTR), Lorenz Andreas Fischer; 47 (UP), Egil Droge/Zambian Carnivore Programme; 47 (LO), Stephen Cunliffe; 48-49 (CTR), Matthew S. Becker/Zambian Carnivore Programme; 50 (UP), Michelle Attala; 50 (LO), Eric Isselee/Shutterstock; 51 (UP), George McCarthy/Minden Pictures; 51 (LO), Julie Lubick/Shutterstock; 52 (CTR), Stephen Cunliffe; 53 (LO), Dale Morris; 54 (UP LE), Maggy Meyer/Shutterstock; 54 (UP CTR LE), Chris Kruger/Shutterstock; 54 (UP CTR), Heinrich Van Den Berg/Dreamstime; 54 (UP CTR RT), Tabby Mittins/Shutterstock; 54 (UP LE), Villiers Steyn/Shutterstock; 54 (LO CTR LE), Nico Smit/Dreamstime; 54 (LO CTR), YolandaVanNiekerk/iStockphoto; 54 (LO CTR LE), EcoPrint/Shutterstock; 54 (LO RT), Pal Teravagimov/Shutterstock; 54 (LO LE), PHOTOCREO Michal Bednarek/Shutterstock; 54 (LO CTR RT), Catherine Falconer/Dreamstime; 55 (LO), Paul Godard